MANCHES
AND
ASHTON UNDER LYNE
TROLLEYBUSES

Stephen Lockwood

Editor Robert J Harley

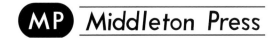

MP Middleton Press

Front cover
This view shows the Manchester trolleybus in all its glory. BUT no 1344 is the only one of the 62-strong final batch of trolleybuses dating from 1955 to survive. It was 'Manchester's last trolleybus' in December 1966 and, together with Ashton's last trolleybus, BUT 87, is currently housed at the East Anglian Transport Museum near Lowestoft, where it is seen in passenger carrying operation on 12th September 2009. (CF Isgar)

Back Cover
Main Photograph: Vehicles from all the three municipal authorities involved in the Manchester and Ashton trolleybus network are shown here together in Stalybridge bus station. See photograph 7 for further information. (CWRouth, colour added by MM Fraser)

Upper left: Ashton 53 was one of eight Crossley vehicles delivered in 1940. Seen in the early 1950s at Stalybridge terminus, it displays the original Ashton livery of dark blue, red and white. It has been modernised with separate route number and destination indicators.
(RF Mack, colour added by MM Fraser)

Upper right: This is one of Manchester's initial fleet of 6-wheel trolleybuses, Leyland TTB4 1070, seen in early wartime posed at Rochdale Road garage. The vehicle is in the full pre-war streamlined livery, but with a grey roof instead of white due to wartime conditions. The destination blinds are set for a service 31X short working journey on Ashton Old Road, (ie turning at Fairfield Road or Grey Mare Lane), which until 1948 was the designation for these services. Service 31, however, to Audenshaw Road The Trough, was renumbered to 29X in 1943. (GMTS, colour added by MM Fraser)

Abbreviations used throughout the text -

BUT   British United Traction. (formerly a trolleybus chassis manufacturer)
GMTS Greater Manchester Transport Society. (a volunteer charity operating the Greater Manchester Museum of Transport)
SHMD Stalybridge, Hyde, Mossley and Dukinfield Joint Transport Board. (formerly a municipal bus operator in north east Cheshire)
UDC   Urban District Council. (a former type of local government district, abolished in 1974.)

Published April 2010

ISBN 978 1 906008 73 4

© *Middleton Press, 2010*

Design Deborah Esher

Published by
    Middleton Press
    Easebourne Lane
    Midhurst
    West Sussex
    GU29 9AZ
Tel: 01730 813169
Fax: 01730 812601
Email: info@middletonpress.co.uk
www.middletonpress.co.uk

Printed in the United Kingdom by Henry Ling Limited, at the Dorset Press, Dorchester, DT1 1HD

CONTENTS

INTRODUCTION AND ACKNOWLEDGEMENTS

For almost thirty years during the middle decades of the twentieth century, the major city of Manchester, together with its much smaller neighbour Ashton under Lyne, operated joint trolleybus services, one of the few such arrangements in Britain. The Manchester system alone was one of the largest in the country, running almost 200 vehicles at its peak in the early 1950s. Despite this, the trolleybuses provided only a fraction of the city's transport needs, the fleet total being less than 15% of the whole of the municipal bus fleet at that time. Amongst its special features was the provision of all-night trolleybus services. 25 years after the demise of the Manchester trolleybuses, electric street traction returned to the streets of the city in the form of the Metrolink trams, whose network, at the date of this book's publication, is being significantly expanded, including a route along the former trolleybus corridor on Ashton New Road to Droylsden due to open in 2012. An onward extension to Ashton under Lyne is planned in due course.

This book provides a pictorial overview of the trolleybus network, giving a glimpse of each route and the vehicles that ran on them. It starts with Ashton's first trolleybus venture with the neighbouring town of Oldham, and progresses to the joint Ashton and Manchester routes, as well as Manchester's exclusive services.

Readers whose interest is kindled by these pages, and who require further detailed historical information, are directed to the definitive historical work on the subject 'The Manchester Trolleybus' by Chris Heaps and Michael Eyre, published by Ian Allan.

Grateful acknowledgement is given for the support and co-operation of all the following individuals who have assisted in the compilation of this book. Roger Smith has specially produced the comprehensive system chronology and wiring maps. These have been drawn using several sources of information to ensure maximum accuracy. The aforementioned Michael Eyre and Chris Heaps, assisted by Keith Walker, have cast critical eyes over my text, and suggested several amendments and clarifications. Peter Thompson, prolific photographer of Manchester's buses, has provided many of his views and made available photographs taken by the late Ray Dunning. He has also provided other relevant information, and has read my text and commented accordingly. Carl Isgar, editor of the National Trolleybus Association's journal 'Trolleybus Magazine' and a native of Manchester, has similarly commented on my text and provided the photograph used on the front cover. Malcolm Fraser MBE has coloured the images used on the rear cover, enabling rare glimpses of former liveries. Terry Russell has allowed the reproduction of his trolleybus drawings, producing the Ashton BUT drawing specially for this book. Other individuals and organisations who have kindly responded to my specific requests for photographs and other items are – Greater Manchester Transport Society, Stephen Howarth, Ted Jones, Stanley King, Stan Ledgard, Manchester Libraries, Eric Old, Robin Symons of the National Trolleybus Association and Paul Watson. Thanks go to all.

Unfortunately it has not been possible to identify the origin of a small number of the photographs, and any further information about these would be welcomed by the author. Any errors and omissions in the text are entirely the author's responsibility.

Finally, I wish to thank my wife Eileen for her patience, support and assistance during the preparation of this book.

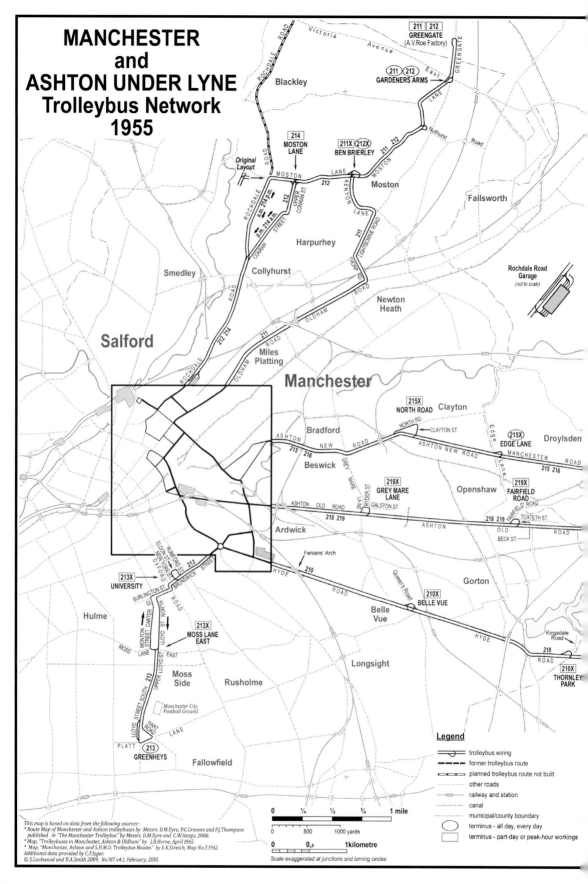

MANCHESTER and ASHTON UNDER LYNE Trolleybus Network 1955

Blackley

| 211 | 212 |
GREENGATE
(A.V.Roe Factory)

(211) (212)
GARDENERS ARMS

| 214 |
MOSTON LANE

| 211X | 212X |
BEN BRIERLEY

Nuthurst

Failsworth

Original Layout

MOSTON LANE

212

Moston

am 214 pm

pm 214 am 212

UPPER CONRAN ST.

CONRAN STREET

212

KENYON LANE

211

LIGHTBOWNE ROAD

Harpurhey

Smedley

Collyhurst

Newton Heath

Rochdale Road Garage
(not to scale)

212 214

211

OLDHAM ROAD

ROCHDALE ROAD

Salford

Miles Platting

Manchester

| 215X |
NORTH ROAD

Clayton

CLAYTON ST.

NORTH RD.

(215X)
EDGE LANE

Droylsden

Bradford

ASHTON NEW ROAD

215 216

ASHTON NEW ROAD

215 216

MANCHESTER ROAD

Edge Lane

Beswick

GREY MARE LANE

RYDER ST.

| 219X |
GREY MARE LANE

GALSTON ST.

Openshaw

| 219X |
FAIRFIELD ROAD

FAIRFIELD ROAD

ASHTON OLD ROAD

218 219

218 219

ASHTON OLD ROAD

TOXTETH ST.

BECK ST.

Ardwick

Fenians' Arch

210

HYDE ROAD

Queen's Road

| 210X |
BELLE VUE

Gorton

| 213X |
UNIVERSITY

ELDON STREET

RUMFORD ST.

OXFORD ROAD

213

BRUNSWICK STREET

BURLINGTON ST.

LLOYD ST NORTH

Hulme

MOSS STREET

CARTER ST.

| 213X |
MOSS LANE EAST

MOSS LANE

LLOYD ST EAST

Belle Vue

Kingsdale Road

HYDE ROAD

210

210 ROAD

| 210X |
THORNLEY PARK

Longsight

213

UPPER LLOYD STREET

Moss Side

Rusholme

Manchester City Football Ground

HART ROAD

LLOYD STREET SOUTH

PLATT LANE

(213)
GREENHEYS

Fallowfield

Legend

	trolleybus wiring
---	former trolleybus route
	planned trolleybus route not built
	other roads
	railway and station
	canal
	municipal/county boundary
	terminus - all day, every day
	terminus - part-day or peak-hour workings

Scale:
0 ¼ ½ ¾ 1 mile
0 500 1000 yards
0 0,5 1kilometre

Scale exaggerated at junctions and turning circles

This map is based on data from the following sources:-
* Route Map of Manchester and Ashton trolleybuses by Messrs. D.M.Eyre, P.G.Greaves and P.J.Thompson
  published in "The Manchester Trolleybus" by Messrs. D.M.Eyre and C.W.Heaps, 2008.
* Map, "Trolleybuses in Manchester, Ashton & Oldham" by J.B.Horne, April 1965.
* Map, "Manchester, Ashton and S.H.M.D. Trolleybus Routes" by E.K.Stretch, Map No.3 1962.
Additional data provided by C.F.Isgar.
© S.Lockwood and R.A.Smith 2009. No.917 v4.1, February, 2010.

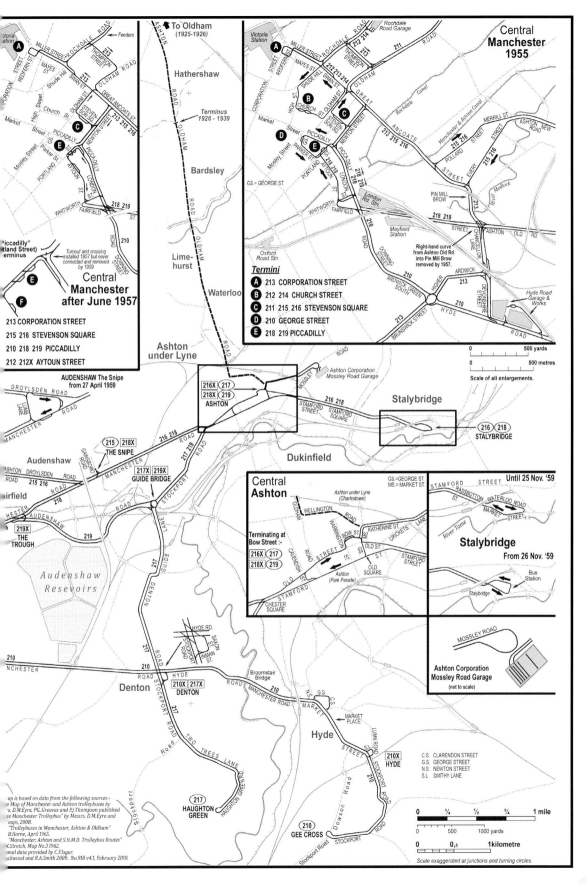

To Oldham (1925-1926)

Hathershaw

Terminus 1926 - 1939

Bardsley

Limehurst

Waterloo

Central Manchester 1955

Termini
- **A** 213 CORPORATION STREET
- **B** 212 214 CHURCH STREET
- **C** 211 215 216 STEVENSON SQUARE
- **D** 210 GEORGE STREET
- **E** 218 219 PICCADILLY

GS. = GEORGE ST.

Right-hand curve from Ashton Old Rd. into Pin Mill Brow removed by 1957.

Hyde Road Garage & Works

Turnout and crossing installed 1957 but never connected and removed by 1959

Central Manchester after June 1957

213 CORPORATION STREET
215 216 STEVENSON SQUARE
210 218 219 PICCADILLY
212 212X AYTOUN STREET

"Piccadilly" (Portland Street) Terminus

AUDENSHAW The Snipe from 27 April 1959

DROYLSDEN ROAD
LUMB LANE

Audenshaw

215 218X THE SNIPE

217X 219X GUIDE BRIDGE

219X THE TROUGH

Audenshaw Reservoirs

Ashton under Lyne

216X 217
218X 219
ASHTON

Ashton Corporation Mossley Road Garage

216 218
STAMFORD STREET STAMFORD SQUARE

Stalybridge

216 218 STALYBRIDGE

Dukinfield

Central Ashton

GS.=GEORGE ST.
MS. = MARKET ST.

Ashton under Lyne (Charlestown)

Terminating at Bow Street :-
216X 217
218X 219

Ashton (Park Parade)

CHESTER SQUARE

Denton

210X 217X DENTON

HYDE RD.
SAXON ST.
INMAN ST.

Broomstair Bridge

Hyde

MARKET PLACE

210X HYDE

C.S. CLARENDON STREET
G.S. GEORGE STREET
N.S. NEWTON STREET
S.L. SMITHY LANE

Until 25 Nov. '59

STAMFORD STREET
RASSBOTTOM ST.
WATERLOO ROAD
MARKET STREET

River Tame

Stalybridge
From 26 Nov. '59

Bus Station

Stalybridge

Ashton Corporation Mossley Road Garage (not to scale)

MOSSLEY ROAD

217 HAUGHTON GREEN

210 GEE CROSS

Map is based on data from the following sources:-
Map of Manchester and Ashton trolleybuses by
D.M.Eyre, PG.Greaves and P.J.Thompson published
the Manchester Trolleybus" by Messrs. D.M.Eyre and
eaps, 2008.
"Trolleybuses in Manchester, Ashton & Oldham"
B.Horne, April 1965.
"Manchester, Ashton and S.H.M.D. Trolleybus Routes"
K.Stretch, Map No.3 1962.
nal data provided by C.F.Isgar.
ckwood and R.A.Smith 2009. No.918 v4.1, February 2010.

0   500 yards
0   500 metres
Scale of all enlargements.

0   ¼   ½   ¾   1 mile
0   500   1000 yards
0   0,5   1kilometre

Scale exaggerated at junctions and turning circles.

GEOGRAPHICAL SETTING

In the period covered by this book, Manchester was in the county of Lancashire and is situated on the River Irwell. On its western and north western boundary was the neighbouring City of Salford. Manchester's greatness is founded on the Lancashire textile industry, notably cotton. Indeed, during the Industrial Revolution, it was known as 'Cottonopolis'. Its importance is reflected by its transport links – it was the terminus of the Liverpool and Manchester Railway opened in 1830, the world's first large scale application of the passenger carrying railway. In 1894 the 36 mile/57km Manchester Ship Canal was opened, allowing sea-going ships to dock in the city. Today, Manchester is part of the Greater Manchester conurbation, which also includes the neighbouring former towns and cities in the area, such as Salford, Oldham, Ashton and Stalybridge.

HISTORICAL BACKGROUND

The first trolleybuses in the area were introduced by Ashton and Oldham Corporations together on 26th August 1925, when the trams operating on their joint service between Ashton and Oldham were replaced by ten Railless type trolleybuses running between Ashton Market Place and Oldham Star Inn. This came about because of the need to renew the tram tracks in Oldham Road, Ashton. Oldham was persuaded to run the joint service with Ashton, but retained the tram tracks within its own boundary as far as Hathershaw in order to continue running its own Hathershaw – Oldham – Summit tram service. Thus Oldham only had two trolleybuses, compared to Ashton's eight, which it needed to run to Oldham, plus the Ashton to Hathershaw local service.

The new service attracted complaints from residents along the route about the vibration and damage to houses caused by the solid tyred vehicles, as well as unreliability (Oldham had no spare trolleybus). After just over a year of operation Oldham pulled out of the arrangement and its last trolleybus ran on 4th September 1926, after which the joint service was run with the motorbuses of both Corporations. Both Oldham vehicles were stored for some time before being broken up, the spare parts being purchased by Ashton. However, Ashton persevered, and maintained the local Hathershaw trolleybus service with its single deck vehicles until they were worn out, being replaced by buses after 19th February 1939.

By this time, other trolleybus developments had taken place. In the 1930s Manchester was looking to convert its vast tram system to bus operation, in particular the route along Ashton Old Road. The Corporation's Transport Committee and management were firmly in favour of oil-engined vehicles, but the City Council wanted to continue to use its own municipal electricity, produced using coal from Lancashire pits. A battle ensued between the two factions, but the will of the full Council prevailed.

Despite not having its way, the Transport Department set about creating a top class trolleybus system, including a brand new garage for 115 vehicles at Rochdale Road. Other municipal operators also became involved. Ashton willingly agreed to run a joint service of trolleybuses from Manchester to Ashton and the Stalybridge, Mossley, Hyde and Dukinfield Joint Transport Board (SHMD) became the third partner, persuading Manchester and Ashton to extend the trolleybuses over its territory into Stalybridge. In the event SHMD eventually declined to operate vehicles, but it did maintain the overhead in its own area, which comprised the portion of the route in Cheshire.

The Ashton Old Road trolleybus service (28) opened on 1st March 1938, enabling Ashton to abandon tram operation altogether. The Ashton New Road tram route to Ashton, operated solely by Manchester (but still regarded as a 'joint' service), was added to the scheme, and Manchester trolleybuses took over in July 1938, these also being extended to Stalybridge (service 26).

The Ashton area trolleybus network was completed by the end of 1940. A route branching off from the Ashton Old Road service at 'The Trough' junction to Guide Bridge reached Ashton in March 1940 (service 29), and a service south from Ashton, via Guide Bridge to Denton and Haughton Green (service 57) was fully open by the end of that year. Both these services were converted from motorbuses, and the 57, although a joint Ashton / Manchester operation, did not go anywhere near Manchester city centre.

Meanwhile, a trolleybus service completely within the city had commenced in April 1940, this being service 30, which replaced trams between the city end of Rochdale Road and the University near Oxford Road.

One other tram route which had been earmarked for trolleybus operation was the nine-mile long service to Hyde which would be run jointly with SHMD. However, wartime necessities meant that these plans were shelved, and instead the decision was taken to use trolleybuses to replace motorbuses as a fuel saving measure. The bus routes concerned ran past, or close to, Rochdale Road garage and the Moston Lane area. The services to Moston were introduced progressively over a period from November 1940 to July 1942, eventually reaching a terminal point at the Gardeners Arms. In 1943 this was extended a short distance beyond the city boundary to the AV Roe aircraft factory at Chadderton for use by peak hour services.

Trolleybus development now slowed, the only further expansion in the 1940s being to the University service 30, which was extended southwards along Lloyd Street South to Platt Lane in 1946, and in 1948 its Rochdale Road terminus was replaced by a more convenient one near Victoria station at Corporation Street, the wiring being extended along Miller Street.

A long awaited delivery of new Crossley trolleybuses finally enabled the Hyde Road route to be converted to trolleybuses in January 1950. The vehicles took over from motorbuses that had replaced the trams in 1948, despite the trolleybus overhead being in place well before then. The route was extended beyond Hyde to Gee Cross. Between Broomstair Bridge, west of Hyde, and Gee Cross the overhead was maintained by the SHMD undertaking. The service was numbered 210, starting a new numbering sequence for trolleybus routes, and over the next four years all existing trolleybus services would be re numbered into the series between 211 and 219. It should be noted here that Manchester's practice was to display the suffix 'X' on any journey or service that did not travel the full distance of the route. Thus trolleybuses turning at Denton, part way along the Gee Cross route, displayed '210X'. Ashton did not use this system.

Principal trolleybus services as at 1st January 1950

Service no	Destination	Terminal Point	New service no	Date renumbered
17	Haughton Green	Ashton	217	1950
26	Stalybridge	Stevenson Square	216	1950
27 (n)	Audenshaw The Snipe	Stevenson Square	215	1950
27X	Edge Lane	Stevenson Square	215X	1950
28	Stalybridge	Portland Street	218	1950
28X(n)	Audenshaw The Snipe	Portland Street	218X	1950
29	Ashton via Guide Bridge	Portland Street	219	1950
30	Platt Lane	Corporation Street	213	1952
31	Gardeners Arms	Stevenson Square	211	1953
31X	Ben Brierley	Stevenson Square	211X	1953
32 (n)	Gardeners Arms	Church Street	212	1953
33	Ben Brierley	Church Street	212X	1953
34	Moston Lane	Church Street	214	1953

Note : Service 17 had been renumbered from 57 in 1947
Services 31 and 31x had been renumbered from 36 and 37 in 1948
(n) denotes this service was also an 'all night' service.

The trolleybus network had now reached its maximum extent of 44 route miles/70 km, operated by 213 vehicles, of which Ashton contributed 24.

Having reached its peak, the system now faced a slow decline. The Moston services, on which the vehicles and infrastructure were in dire need of replacement, were converted back to motorbus operation in two stages. First to go were the Rochdale Road routes in April 1955, followed by those along Oldham Road in August of that year. One note of optimism was the entry into service of 62 new BUT trolleybuses for Manchester and eight in Ashton in 1955/6. Meanwhile, Rochdale Road garage lost its remaining trolleybuses in April 1956, after which all Manchester's trolleybuses were housed at Hyde Road garage.

The period from April 1956 to May 1959 was one of relative calm, and was characterised by changes to wiring layouts at Piccadilly and Audenshaw due to one way traffic schemes being introduced in these areas.

However, the firm intention was to gradually end trolleybus operation as soon as the loans taken out on the vehicles and infrastructure were paid off. Major building work at the area around the 213 city terminus caused the conversion of the whole route to motorbuses in May 1959, followed in the July of 1960 by the conversion of the Haughton Green service, due to large housing development in the Haughton Green area.

By this time, Ashton had changed its mind about running trolleybuses, and urged Manchester to close the joint Ashton services. Manchester, who planned to continue operations until 1967 when the BUT vehicles would be debt free, was more concerned about events elsewhere. In April 1963 the Hyde service was changed to motorbuses, due to the desire to extend services in the area, thereby thwarting the ambitions of another bus operator. One Ashton service, the 219, did end in October 1964 as a result of pending major road works at Chester Square in Ashton.

The next two years saw the final run down of trolleybus operations. The surviving all-night service 215X had already finished in mid-1964, followed by the takeover of some Sunday trolleybus operations by motorbuses. Manchester's entire share of the 218 went over to motorbuses in May 1966, leaving only Ashton trolleybuses on the Ashton Old Road corridor. At the end of August trolleybuses ceased to run on Saturdays, and the final closure of the system was planned to take place on Friday 30th December 1966. Manchester's plans to commemorate the event, by placing full colour posters in every vehicle, were upset at the last minute by a printers' strike but the closure went ahead as scheduled. The last vehicles on Ashton New Road were 1321 and 1354 running together and a trolleybus (1302) was turned out instead of the usual motorbus to run the last 218X journey of the day along Ashton Old Road to Audenshaw, something that had not happened for many months. Slightly earlier that evening, Ashton's official last trolleybus, 87, adorned with commemorative posters, followed behind Ashton's last scheduled trolleybus journey which was being operated by 83. The pair ran from Piccadilly to Stalybridge and back to Ashton garage. On the following day the operation of enthusiasts' tours was generously allowed by Manchester (see the Finale section at the end of the book), and this was the last time (up to the present…!) that trolleybuses have run on Manchester's streets.

MANCHESTER, ASHTON UNDER LYNE and OLDHAM
Trolleybus Chronology

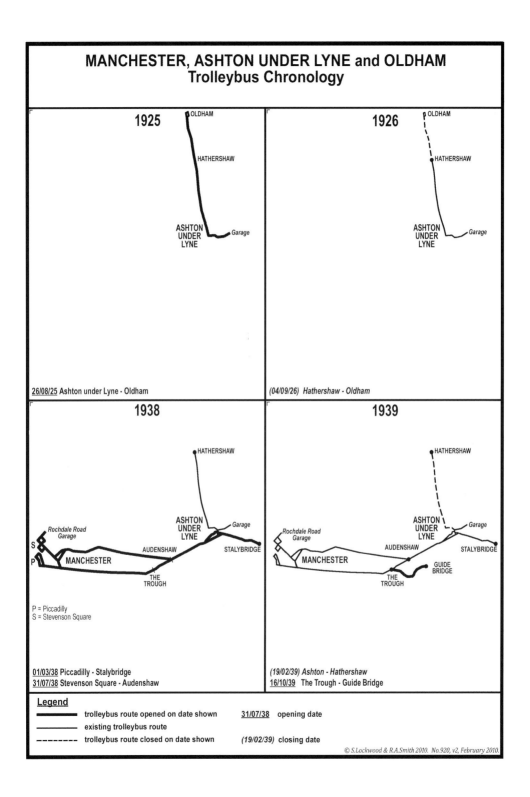

1925

OLDHAM
HATHERSHAW
ASHTON UNDER LYNE — Garage

26/08/25 Ashton under Lyne - Oldham

1926

OLDHAM
HATHERSHAW
ASHTON UNDER LYNE — Garage

(04/09/26) Hathershaw - Oldham

1938

HATHERSHAW
ASHTON UNDER LYNE — Garage
Rochdale Road Garage
S
P
MANCHESTER
AUDENSHAW
STALYBRIDGE
THE TROUGH

P = Piccadilly
S = Stevenson Square

01/03/38 Piccadilly - Stalybridge
31/07/38 Stevenson Square - Audenshaw

1939

HATHERSHAW
ASHTON UNDER LYNE — Garage
Rochdale Road Garage
MANCHESTER
AUDENSHAW
STALYBRIDGE
GUIDE BRIDGE
THE TROUGH

(19/02/39) Ashton - Hathershaw
16/10/39 The Trough - Guide Bridge

Legend

⸺	trolleybus route opened on date shown
—	existing trolleybus route
- - - - -	trolleybus route closed on date shown

31/07/38 opening date
(19/02/39) closing date

MANCHESTER, ASHTON UNDER LYNE and OLDHAM
Trolleybus Chronology

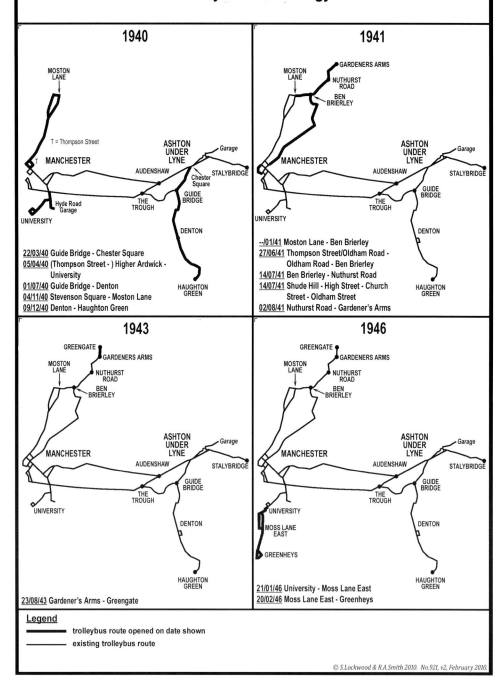

1940

22/03/40 Guide Bridge - Chester Square
05/04/40 (Thompson Street -) Higher Ardwick - University
01/07/40 Guide Bridge - Denton
04/11/40 Stevenson Square - Moston Lane
09/12/40 Denton - Haughton Green

1941

--/01/41 Moston Lane - Ben Brierley
27/06/41 Thompson Street/Oldham Road - Oldham Road - Ben Brierley
14/07/41 Ben Brierley - Nuthurst Road
14/07/41 Shude Hill - High Street - Church Street - Oldham Street
02/08/41 Nuthurst Road - Gardener's Arms

1943

23/08/43 Gardener's Arms - Greengate

1946

21/01/46 University - Moss Lane East
20/02/46 Moss Lane East - Greenheys

Legend

━━━━ trolleybus route opened on date shown
──── existing trolleybus route

MANCHESTER, ASHTON UNDER LYNE and OLDHAM
Trolleybus Chronology

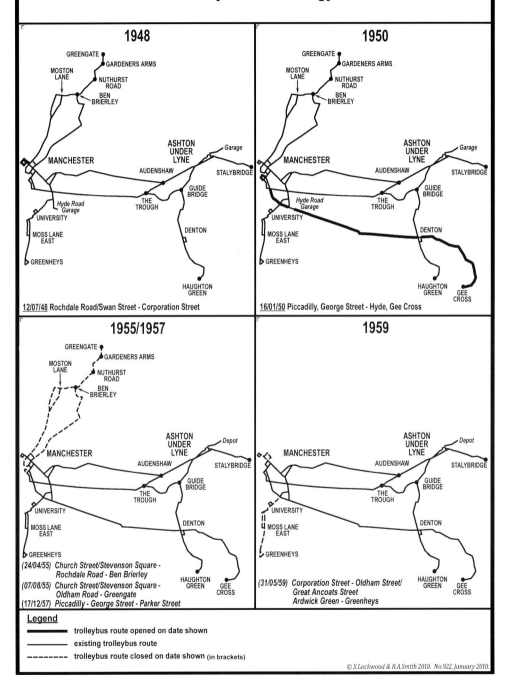

1948

12/07/48 Rochdale Road/Swan Street - Corporation Street

1950

16/01/50 Piccadilly, George Street - Hyde, Gee Cross

1955/1957

(24/04/55) Church Street/Stevenson Square -
Rochdale Road - Ben Brierley
(07/08/55) Church Street/Stevenson Square -
Oldham Road - Greengate
(17/12/57) Piccadilly - George Street - Parker Street

1959

(31/05/59) Corporation Street - Oldham Street/
Great Ancoats Street
Ardwick Green - Greenheys

Legend

▬▬▬ trolleybus route opened on date shown
───── existing trolleybus route
------- trolleybus route closed on date shown (in brackets)

© S.Lockwood & R.A.Smith 2010. No.922, January 2010.

MANCHESTER, ASHTON UNDER LYNE and OLDHAM
Trolleybus Chronology

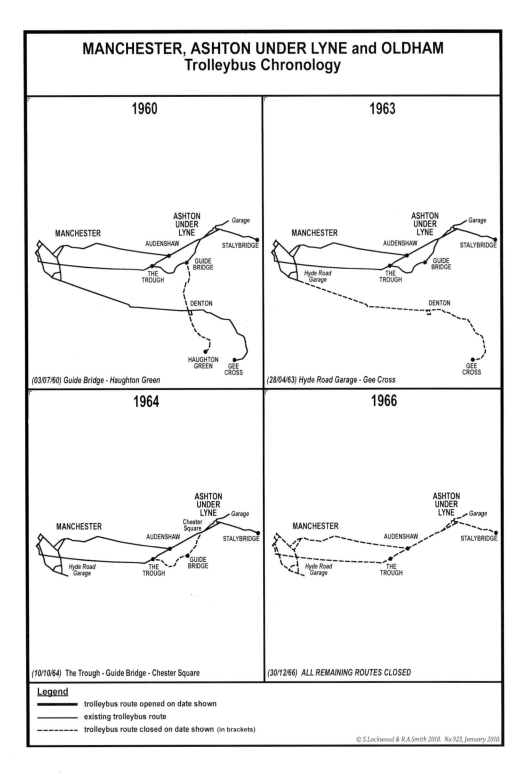

1960

ASHTON UNDER LYNE — Garage
MANCHESTER
AUDENSHAW
STALYBRIDGE
GUIDE BRIDGE
THE TROUGH
DENTON
HAUGHTON GREEN
GEE CROSS

(03/07/60) Guide Bridge - Haughton Green

1963

ASHTON UNDER LYNE — Garage
MANCHESTER
AUDENSHAW
STALYBRIDGE
GUIDE BRIDGE
Hyde Road Garage
THE TROUGH
DENTON
GEE CROSS

(28/04/63) Hyde Road Garage - Gee Cross

1964

ASHTON UNDER LYNE — Garage
Chester Square
MANCHESTER
AUDENSHAW
STALYBRIDGE
GUIDE BRIDGE
Hyde Road Garage
THE TROUGH

(10/10/64) The Trough - Guide Bridge - Chester Square

1966

ASHTON UNDER LYNE — Garage
MANCHESTER
AUDENSHAW
STALYBRIDGE
Hyde Road Garage
THE TROUGH

(30/12/66) ALL REMAINING ROUTES CLOSED

Legend

——— trolleybus route opened on date shown
——— existing trolleybus route
- - - - - trolleybus route closed on date shown (in brackets)

© S.Lockwood & R.A.Smith 2010. No.923, January 2010.

OLDHAM TO ASHTON

1.   Ten of these Railless trolley vehicles, with Short Bros 36 seat centre entrance bodies, were bought as one lot in 1925 to operate the Oldham to Ashton service. Two became Oldham 1 and 2, and the other eight became Ashton nos 50 to 57. The reason for the imbalance in the number of vehicles is explained in the 'Historical Background'. This is Oldham 2 seen when new before delivery. Together with its sister vehicle, it was destined for a short operational life, being withdrawn in September 1926 when Oldham abandoned trolleybus operation. (R Marshall collection)

2.   Ashton Railless vehicle 51 is seen on a trial run shortly before the opening of the Oldham to Ashton service in August 1925. It is at Hathershaw, on the Ashton – Oldham boundary. In the background is an Oldham Corporation tram on the Hathershaw–Oldham-Summit service 7, which continued to operate after the trolleybuses were introduced. Note that unlike Manchester's practice when trolleybuses started running there, the tram is sharing the same overhead as the trolleybus. (D Randall / AE Old)

3.   Following Oldham's withdrawal from trolleybus operation in September 1926, Ashton continued to run its vehicles as far as the boundary at Hathershaw, where there was a turning circle at the junction of Ashton Road with Pelham Street. This view shows the terminus in 1938, shortly before the service ceased. Railless car 56, rebuilt with rear entrance and pneumatic tyres, waits before returning to Ashton. (WA Camwell, National Tramway Museum)

4.   The trolleybus route in Ashton was used in the late 1930s to test prototype vehicles built by Crossley motors, as well as Manchester's first operational trolleybus (1006). This 1937 scene in Wellington Road Ashton, near the Town Hall, shows Ashton Railless vehicle 54 about to pass the prototype Crossley 4-wheel trolleybus. This vehicle was purchased by Ashton later in 1937, becoming 49 in the fleet. (Crossley Motors)

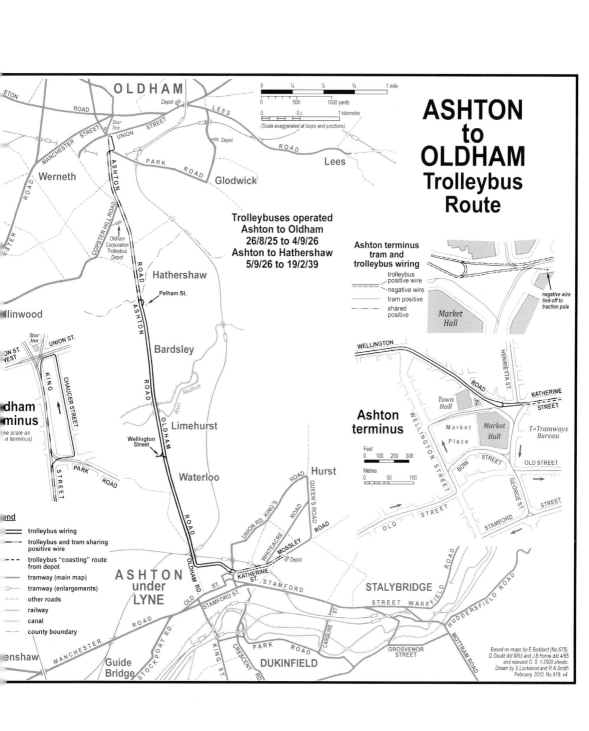

ASHTON to OLDHAM
Trolleybus Route

Trolleybuses operated
Ashton to Oldham
26/8/25 to 4/9/26
Ashton to Hathershaw
5/9/26 to 19/2/39

Ashton terminus tram and trolleybus wiring

- trolleybus positive wire
- negative wire
- tram positive
- shared positive

negative wire tied-off to traction pole

Ashton terminus

Feet
0 100 200 300

Metres
0 50 100

T=Tramways Bureau

Oldham terminus
(same scale as Ashton terminus)

Legend

- trolleybus wiring
- trolleybus and tram sharing positive wire
- trolleybus "coasting" route from depot
- tramway (main map)
- tramway (enlargements)
- other roads
- railway
- canal
- county boundary

Based on maps by E.Beddard (No.675), D.Gould d/d 9/03 and J.B.Horne d/d 4/65 and relevant O. S. 1.2500 sheets. Drawn by S.Lockwood and R.A.Smith February, 2010, No.919, v4.

Scale markers: ¼ ½ ¾ 1 mile; 500 1000 yards; 0.5 1 kilometre
(Scale exaggerated at loops and junctions)

Place names: OLDHAM, Werneth, Glodwick, Lees, Hathershaw, Pelham St., Bardsley, Limehurst, Waterloo, Hurst, ASHTON under LYNE, STALYBRIDGE, DUKINFIELD, Guide Bridge, Collinwood, Market Hall, Town Hall, Market Place

5.　　　The Ashton terminus was at the Tramways Bureau, an office-cum-shelter building outside the Town Hall. Here Railless 57 stands before commencing a journey to Hathershaw. The sign on the left above the vehicle reads 'Trolley Buses leave here for Waterloo, Bardsley and Hathershaw'. The Tramways Bureau survived as a bus terminus into the 1960s before being demolished, although the later trolleybus services did not use it. (R Marshall collection)

STALYBRIDGE

6.   The town of Stalybridge was part of Cheshire in trolleybus days and is close to the Pennine moors and hills. It was the terminus of the eight mile long routes 216 and 218 from Manchester. The trolleybuses used a clockwise loop through the town centre streets. The terminal stand, seen here, was in Waterloo Road, outside the SHMD general offices building. In the late 1950s, Manchester BUT 1325 waits here before returning to the big city via Ashton Old Road. (C Carter)

7.   In November 1959, a bus station was opened in Stalybridge at King Street. Trolleybuses were diverted to terminate at the western side of the station from 26th November, and this necessitated changing the terminal loop to operate in the opposite direction, ie anti-clockwise. The eastern end of the loop, beyond King Street, was abandoned completely. This early 1960s view shows trolleybuses in Stalybridge bus station, and it depicts vehicles from all the three municipal participants of the trolleybus operation. Ashton BUT 83 is in the foreground, with Manchester BUT 1326 in the background. On the left is the SHMD Thornycroft tower wagon, which was used to maintain the trolleybus overhead between here and the Ashton boundary at Stamford Park. (CW Routh)

8.　　On leaving the bus station, trolleybuses turned left into Waterloo Road where Manchester BUT 1337 is seen on 29th April 1962. The wiring turning out of the bus station is visible in the right background. Before 1959, the route ran in the opposite direction along here, and the terminus was in the far distance. Stalybridge Fire Station is on the left. (AD Packer)

9.　　Trolleybuses entered Stalybridge via Rassbottom Street, the one way loop commencing at the railway bridge situated at the bottom of this street. Ashton BUT 89, the final trolleybus purchased by the corporation, emerges from under the bridge and will proceed into Market Street. It is about to negotiate the crossing with the return wiring coming in from the right (Waterloo Road). The entrance to Stalybridge railway station is just beyond the bridge on the left. The station is on the main line between Manchester and Leeds via Huddersfield, which in trolleybus days ran from Manchester Exchange Station via Ashton. It burrows under the Pennines by the three mile long Standedge tunnel, one of the longest in Britain. (DF Parker)

10.   The long climb out of Stalybridge, up Rassbottom Street, was one of the steepest gradients on the Ashton / Manchester trolleybus system. Manchester BUT 1323 is seen here on a journey to Stevenson Square on service 216, against a backdrop of the Stalybridge roof tops and the Pennine hills above Longdendale. The overhead wiring here is suspended from SHMD tram poles, the one on the left still carrying its ornate finial. (JS King)

11.   At the top of Rassbottom Street is Thompson Cross, where the trolleybuses bore left on to Stamford Street to proceed into Ashton. This scene is on Stamford Street at the Ashton / Stalybridge boundary, (and, in trolleybus days, the Lancashire / Cheshire boundary). Ashton Crossley 79 is about to cross into Lancashire proceeding towards Ashton. SHMD tram poles are in evidence, whilst the one in the immediate left foreground is an Ashton Corporation tram pole. (JS King)

STAMFORD PARK

12.   Ashton's main recreational park is Stamford Park, which straddled the Ashton / Stalybridge boundary. At weekends and holidays, substantial numbers of visitors were carried to and from the park by the trolleybuses, and a large waiting shelter, seen here, was provided. Manchester BUT 1329 is picking up a passenger on its way into Ashton on a day when visitors to the park would have been few and far between. (CW Routh)

13. This view at Stamford Park looks towards Stalybridge. There was no wiring provision for trolleybuses to turn here, although they sometimes did so by using their traction battery facility to reverse into Mellor Road beside the Sycamore public house. One such occasion was on 10th October 1964, when for some reason trolleybuses were unable to run into Stalybridge. Ashton 61, one of the wartime Sunbeam W vehicles re bodied by Roe in 1958, is about to reverse into Mellor Road, whilst Manchester's highest numbered trolleybus, 1362, waits its turn in front. Prior to being re bodied, Ashton 61 would not have been able to manoeuvre on battery power. (RDH Symons)

14. This is another view taken on the same day as the previous photograph, and shows Ashton BUT 82 using battery traction to cross back into Stamford Street after having reversed into Mellor Road. Passengers wait for this process to be completed. (RDH Symons)

ASHTON TOWN CENTRE

15.   In Ashton town centre, between St Michael's Square in the east and Henry Square in the west, trolleybuses used a one way route in either direction. Westbound towards Manchester, the route kept to Stamford Street throughout. At Old Square, Manchester Leyland TB5 trolleybus 1104, one of a batch of 37 delivered in 1940, stands at the loading point for service 216 beside Yates's Wine Lodge on 16th July 1955. The driver has turned round to watch the Saturday afternoon shoppers climb aboard. In the far background, behind the Vauxhall saloon car can be seen one of Ashton's post war Crossley trolleybuses emerging from St Michael's Square, where the Stalybridge bound wires rejoin Stamford Street. The wires trailing in at Old Square from George Street, were used by vehicles starting their journeys at Ashton Market Place to return towards Manchester or Haughton Green. (J Copland / P Watson)

➔ 16. Stamford Street was one of Ashton's main shopping areas. Re-bodied Ashton Sunbeam 61 is seen here proceeding to Manchester via Guide Bridge. Further along the street, there was a wiring junction where a connection led along Cavendish Street to Old Street. This was used by trolleybuses either returning to Ashton garage from the Stalybridge direction, or those running from the garage to enter service at Ashton Market Place. (CW Routh)

↓ 17. Coming from Manchester, the trolleybus route into Ashton turned off Stamford Street at Henry Square, and ran along Old Street and Warrington Street to reach Ashton Market Place. Here, the 216 / 218 Stalybridge services passed through, whilst the 217 from Haughton Green and 219 from Manchester (via Guide Bridge) services terminated. A loop in the wiring allowed through vehicles to pass those terminating here. In this scene, dating from 1964, Ashton BUT 85 is working to Stalybridge passing Manchester BUT 1301 at the 219 terminal stop. (RS Ledgard)

18.   Ashton 1940 vintage Crossley 54 is seen waiting at the 219 stand on 15th August 1958, alongside the market fair attractions. Although this vehicle was one of only two of this type that remained in service after 1956 (running until 1960), it still had no provision to show a service number. Note the lower front panel with ventilation holes, and compare this with that shown on the slightly earlier photograph of the same vehicle seen later in the book (photograph 105). (PJ Thompson)

→   19.   This late 1950s view at the Market Place shows Ashton BUT 84 at the terminal stop for the Haughton Green service. The vehicle still has its original paint style with blue painted corner pillars to the front upper deck windows. This was later changed to cream. (Roy Brook / P Watson)

↓　20.　Bow Street, which ran along the south side of the Market Hall, was where the main loading stop for Stalybridge was situated. From here, all service trolleybuses turned right into Market Street. In 1962, Ashton BUT 89 has just departed from this stop en route to Stalybridge. The overhead wiring turning left into Market Street was part of the connection leading to the garage. The Market Hall was a Grade II listed building and parts of it dated from 1829. Sadly, it was to be completely destroyed by fire in May 2004, but it has now been rebuilt and looks very much the same as the original building. (J Copland / P Watson)

21.   Further along Market Street, Ashton post war Crossley 78, resplendent in the original dark blue, white and red livery, is seen just before turning sharp left outside the Pitt and Nelson Hotel into Old Street to continue towards Stalybridge. The date is Saturday, 16th July 1955. In the background, outside the Market Hall, can be seen one of Ashton's older Crossley vehicles, dating from 1940. The wiring trailing in above 78 is the garage connection, used by trolleybuses entering service. (J Copland / P Watson)

ASHTON GARAGE

22.   Ashton's trolleybuses were housed at the garage in Mossley Road. This was half a mille from the town centre, and away from the service routes. The wiring connection led from Bow Street, via Market Street and Katherine Street to Mossley Road. In this view, post war Crossley 81 is returning to the garage and is in Market Street near the former Tramways Bureau, having turned left out of Bow Street. An Ashton BUT can be seen in the right background. Note the traces of the former tram tracks in the road. The motorbus on the left is one of four Guy Arab vehicles fitted with Bond bodywork similar to Ashton's eight BUT trolleybuses. (CW Routh)

23. The garage which housed the trolleybuses was completed in 1902 and it originally accommodated the municipal electric trams. In this late 1950s view, post war Crossley 77 and BUT 83 stand in the forecourt.
(Roy Brook / P Watson)

24. The overhead layout in the depot forecourt was of interest. The loop of wiring leading into the depot forecourt from Mossley Road was physically (though not electrically) separate from the internal depot wires. The trolley poles had to be moved from one set of wires to the other when vehicles entered or left the garage. Rebodied Sunbeam 61 stands in the depot forecourt, showing the electrical connection to each set of wires. (RS Ledgard)

25.   Occasionally, a Manchester trolleybus could be seen at Ashton's garage. This occurred when a breakdown in Ashton's area resulted in a Manchester vehicle being replaced by an Ashton one. On 1st October 1966, Manchester BUT 1334 stands in the forecourt before being returned 'home'. (AD Packer)

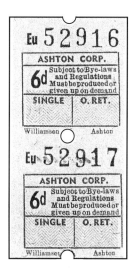

CHESTER SQUARE

26.　　We return now to the trolleybus journey into Manchester. At the west end of Stamford Street is Chester Square, where the direct service 218 diverged from the 219 service via Guide Bridge and the 217 service to Haughton Green. On 11th June 1963, Ashton BUT 83 approaches this point on a 218 journey towards Ashton, and the wires towards Guide Bridge fork left along Stockport Road. In 1965, the road layout at this junction was considerably rebuilt, and during the reconstruction work trolleybuses often had to make in-service battery manoeuvres. (PJ Thompson)

AUDENSHAW

27.　From Chester Square, the 218 trolleybus service ran along Manchester Road, crossing Ashton Moss. At the Snipe Inn, seen on the left, the boundary of Ashton's and Manchester's respective operating territories was reached.　Ashton BUT 85 is seen crossing into Manchester territory and approaching Audenshaw. (C Carter)

28.　Two trolleybus services terminated at Audenshaw (The Snipe) from the Manchester direction. These were the 215 to Stevenson Square, running along Ashton New Road, and the 218X, to Piccadilly along Ashton Old Road. Until 1959, these turned by a means of a reversing triangle at Gainsboro Road, just west of the Snipe Inn.　Pre-war Crossley six-wheeler 1052 is seen having just reversed and parked in Gainsboro Road with the crew posed in front. Note the sign on the pole on the right! 18th June 1955. (R Dunning)

29.   The Snipe triangular reverser is seen here on Sunday, 12th April 1959. BUT 1341 on service 215 has reversed, into Gainsboro Road and is about to pull forward across Manchester Road. The Snipe Inn is in the right background. (PJ Thompson)

(83)   Operation of Overhead Switches

It is the Driver's duty to see that the Conductor is at the pull switch before proceeding through frogs.

Check with indicator light before passing through the frog.

Electrically operated switches are generally set for the straight. To proceed on the straight, the driver should coast through the skate without depressing either foot pedal.

To operate the switch for the curve, the driver MUST TAKE CURRENT on passing through the skate.

All electrically operated switch frogs have illuminated signals fixed on the adjacent poles indicating whether the switch is set for the straight or for the curve. If no illumination is seen, set the frog by hand and notify Breakdowns (ARDwick 3322).

30.   Just west of Gainsboro Road, the trolleybuses passed under a railway bridge, beyond which was the road junction where the routes along Ashton Old and New Roads diverged. From April 1959 this junction was considerably modified, introducing a gyratory traffic system incorporating Lumb Lane. This allowed terminating trolleybuses to turn, and the reversing triangle at the Snipe Inn (the only one on the Manchester system) was removed. Loops in the wiring were provided, both on the gyratory layout and at the terminal stand outside Ryecroft Hall to allow vehicles to pass. In this scene, post war Crossley 1209 is completing its turning manoeuvre and is about to pull onto the terminal stop. It is working on the peak hour service 212X along Ashton Old Road introduced in the late 1950s, which ran to and from Aytoun Street instead of Piccadilly. (J Fozard)

31.   The terminal stop outside Ryecroft Hall (where the Audenshaw Urban District Council offices were based) is seen here. Manchester BUT 1333 on service 215 is overtaking similar vehicle 1309 on service 218X. It will turn right into Lumb Lane to get to Droylsden Road, passing through the automatic frog seen in the foreground. (RS Ledgard)

32.   Although the wiring layout at Ryecroft Hall allowed turns from any direction, it was not normally used by Ashton trolleybuses terminating from the Ashton direction. On this occasion, however, Ashton BUT 82 is seen having just negotiated the automatic frog to turn into Lumb Lane, to allow it to turn back towards Ashton. On this day, 28th November 1965, a Manchester bus strike has resulted in all Ashton vehicles making this manoeuvre. (PJ Thompson)

➔   33. Manchester BUT 1303 is seen making the turn into Lumb Lane at the start of its journey through Droylsden and along Ashton New Road to Stevenson Square. (C Carter)

➔   34. The other 'leg' of the gyratory layout is the eastern end of Droylsden Road. Here, two Manchester BUTs run side by side. On the left, 1362 is about to turn towards the Ryecroft Hall terminus on a terminating 215 journey, whilst 1321 is proceeding towards Ashton on a 216 journey to Stalybridge. (DF Parker)

GUIDE BRIDGE

35.   At Chester Square, Ashton, service 219 branched off along Stockport Road to serve Guide Bridge. Until 1960, service 217 to Haughton Green similarly served Guide Bridge, where it left the 219 wires to run towards Denton. This scene is at Guide Bridge on the last day of trolleybus operation, 10th October 1964, and shows Manchester BUT 1315 approaching the full circle of wiring which allowed turns from any direction. This was the boundary point between Ashton and Manchester maintained wiring. Trolleybuses from Manchester turning here were designated 219X. The Haughton Green route branched off where the photographer is standing (see photograph 56). Note the 'Jubbly' delivery lorry on the right. In the 1950s and '60s, 'Jubbly' was a popular orange drink sold in a distinctive triangular carton, often frozen. (Roy Brook / P Watson)

ASHTON OLD ROAD

36.   Services 218 and 219 ran together from 'The Trough' junction into Manchester. Ashton BUT 86 is seen coasting through the junction wiring on its way to Piccadilly. The loop wiring can be seen in the background, as can the water trough which gives the junction its name. (C Carter)

37.   At Fairfield Wells, Ashton post-war Crossley 80 pauses to pick up passengers. This vehicle was the last of either operator's Crossley trolleybuses to survive in service, and it was subsequently purchased for preservation. It is now on display, although not restored, at the Greater Manchester Museum of Transport. (V Nutton, Travel Lens Photographic)

38.   This interesting scene shows Fairfield Wells not long after the introduction of trolleybuses in 1938. The view looks towards Manchester and shows Crossley trolleybus 1009 on a service 28X journey from Audenshaw. This point was the boundary between the Audenshaw UDC area and Manchester (Openshaw), and where Manchester Road, Audenshaw, becomes Ashton Old Road. On the right was the 'Manchester Corporation Transport Dept. Parcels Receiving Office'. The redundant tram track layout is evident. This had incorporated a 'by-pass' track (seen here on the left) allowing trams passing through this point to proceed without being impeded by those reversing on the crossover. The approaching single deck bus is most probably a 'Yorkshire Traction' Leyland Tiger, operating on the express service over the Pennines to Barnsley.

39.   The Openshaw area, through which Ashton Old Road passed, was highly industrialised, being close to several heavy engineering works. At Fairfield Road, there was another turn-back facility, where wiring looped around narrow side streets on the northern side of Ashton Old Road. Manchester BUT 1359 on a 219X journey to Guide Bridge passes the exit wiring which is emerging from Beck Street.
(C Carter)

40. The first point from the city centre along Ashton Old Road that a trolleybus could turn was at Grey Mare Lane. A loop of wiring was provided via Grey Mare Lane, Galston Street (behind the Grey Mare Hotel), and Ryder Street. In this scene dated Saturday 14th August 1965, BUT 1350 has dewired in Galston Street. (RDH Symons)

41. At Pin Mill Brow, the Ashton Old Road trolleybuses met the 213 service from Corporation Street to Greenheys (see photograph 73). After the abandonment of this route in 1959, the wiring was retained for access to Hyde Road garage. Beyond here, trolleybuses ran along Fairfield Street, adjacent to Manchester London Road railway station. Here, there were three overbridges, two carrying railway tracks and in between them a footbridge giving access from the main station to the Mayfield suburban station which was closed to passengers in August 1960. In mid-1959, the railway bridges were replaced as part of the West Coast main line electrification scheme. This rather bizarre view shows the arrangements in place in Fairfield Street to allow continued trolleybus operation during this process. BUT 1320 is approaching the city centre on a journey from Audenshaw.

42.　　Part of the rebuilt railway station complex, re-named Manchester Piccadilly in September 1960, is evident here. Near the end of trolleybus operation, Ashton BUT 89 is seen on a journey from Piccadilly, having just passed under the only two through platforms at the station. (RF Mack)

(86)　Dewirements

In order to avoid dewirement, drivers should:----
(A) Reduce speed at sharp bends, at railway bridges, turning circles and junctions.
(B) Where possible, drive outside the wires on curves so that the bus describes a larger circle than the trolleys.
(C) When leaving curves or junctions, not increase speed until the trolleys are clear and on the straight.
(D) Not brake violently or accelerate fiercely.
(E) Give due consideration to the condition of the road surface.

The trolley indicator light should be specially observed when passing under section insulators, frogs, crossings and curve lines, and the hand-brake lever should be clasped so that the bus can be stopped immediately should a trolley leave the wire and thus prevent damage to the overhead equipment and to the vehicle.

Particulars of each individual dewirement must be submitted on the forms provided.

In the event of a trolley accident, the bus may be moved a short distance on the battery. Switch off the M.G. set before replacing the trolleys on the overhead lines.

43. At the end of Fairfield Street, trolleybuses turned into London Road, joining the wires of the Hyde Road service 210 trolleybuses. Until 1957 trolleybuses were routed straight ahead at this junction to get to Piccadilly via Aytoun Street. Thereafter, the direction of travel was reversed and trolleybuses used Aytoun Street in the outbound direction. The inbound wiring seen heading across the junction provided a loop around Whitworth Street, avoiding Piccadilly and was used by some peak hour short workings which showed 'London Road' as the terminal point. BUT 1318 is seen about to turn right into London Road towards Piccadilly, beside a British Railways Scammell 'Scarab' mechanical horse. (WJ Haynes)

ASHTON NEW ROAD

44.　　From Audenshaw, the Ashton New Road trolleybuses ran into Stevenson Square via Droylsden. The boundary between Manchester (Clayton) and Droylsden, was at Edge Lane, where Ashton New Road commences. There was a short working turning circle here used by service 215X. This service had an intensive all day 5 minute frequency. Edge Lane itself is on the extreme left, and the view looks along Manchester Road Droylsden towards Audenshaw. Manchester BUT 1359 is on the turning circle, having completed its journey from Stevenson Square. On Manchester Road, heading towards Audenshaw is BUT 1306 working on the Saturday 216X service to Ashton Market Place. Opposite this is Ashton BUT 84, not normally seen on the Ashton New Road section, working on an enthusiasts' tour. The wooden fronted building at the turning circle was a Transport Department office, originally built as a Tramways Parcels Office. 15th April 1962. (JH Turner)

45.   This animated view on Ashton New Road at the junction with North Road, Clayton shows
Leyland 1122 bound for Stalybridge on Saturday 18th June 1955. At this point there was another
turning facility where peak hour short workings terminated and turned by means of a one way loop
around North Road (in the right background) and Clayton Street. Note the cooling towers of the
Stuart Street electricity power station in the left background and the gas lamps on top of the toilet
building on the right. (R Dunning)

46.   Post war 6-wheeler 1246 pauses at the stop on the Clayton turn-back loop in North Road
before returning to Stevenson Square in the early evening of 19th April 1963. This vehicle was
withdrawn in July 1963, two months after the abandonment of the Hyde Road trolleybus services.
(PJ Thompson)

47.   This evocative scene, pictured on 9th June 1966, near the end of trolleybus operations shows Ashton New Road at Bradford, just east of the junction with Forge Lane. BUT 1362 is picking up city bound passengers at the stop, and is being passed by a corporation Leyland motorbus working a service from Droylsden which was run jointly with the well known independent bus operator, A Mayne and Son. In the foreground is a well rusted Ford Anglia car. The imposing looking building in the background is the Beswick Co-operative Society's emporium. (AD Packer)

48.   On the approach to the city centre, the Ashton New Road trolleybuses ran in separate streets to and from Great Ancoats Street. Inbound, they ran along Every Street, whilst outbound vehicles used Pollard Street and Merrill Street. In this view, BUT 1301 is seen in Merrill Street (formerly named Mitchell Street), passing the Salvation Army's Star Hall which was built by Frank Crossley, one of the founders of Crossley Motors. 27th December 1965. (PJ Thompson)

49.   At the western end of Every Street, city bound trolleybuses turned right into Great Ancoats Street. There were also wiring connections to turn left towards Pin Mill Brow and Hyde Road garage. BUT 1301 is seen again, ready to turn right out of Every Street on 9th September 1966. (AD Packer)

50.   BUT 1320, with trolley poles at full stretch, is seen negotiating roadworks in Great Ancoats Street, having just made the turn out of Every Street. Until 1959, these wires were also used by service 213 trolleybuses to and from Greenheys. On the right is the extensive Ancoats railway goods station. 21st June 1966. (PJ Thompson)

HAUGHTON GREEN

51.   After reviewing the routes from Ashton to Manchester, we now turn to The Ashton to Haughton Green service, which although jointly worked by Ashton and Manchester vehicles, did not run to Manchester city centre. The Haughton Green terminus was a quiet area in trolleybus days, and Manchester BUT 1339 is seen about to turn round at the end of Haughton Green Road.
 (Roy Brook / P Watson)

52.   This interesting view dating from the spring of 1956 shows both Manchester and Ashton vehicles at the terminal stop. Manchester BUT 1341 is only a few months old, whilst Ashton 49, standing behind, dates from 1936, being the prototype Crossley 4-wheel trolleybus (see photograph 4). This vehicle would be taken out of service later in 1956 following the delivery of Ashton's own BUT vehicles. (C Carter)

53.   This is Two Trees Lane, one of the suburban streets on the route between the terminus and the main Stockport Road. On 6th May 1960, Ashton Crossley 52 of 1940 is seen near St George's Gardens proceeding towards the terminus on driver training duties. Two of this type survived until the closure of the Haughton Green route in July 1960, only a few months after this view was recorded. The lack of general activity in the street is perhaps due to this day being a national holiday to celebrate the wedding of Princess Margaret. (PJ Thompson)

54.   At Crown Point, Denton, the Haughton Green trolleybuses crossed those on the Hyde service from Manchester. The wiring junction here allowed trolleybuses to turn round from the Ashton or Manchester directions, using a loop of wiring around side streets (see photograph 60). Manchester and Ashton BUTs 1324 and 83 respectively are waiting to cross Hyde Road from the Guide Bridge direction on 30th December 1959. No 1324 is showing 217X and is working on a lunchtime advertised extra journey to Haughton Green which commenced at Guide Bridge at 12.25pm. Note the Ford Prefect car alongside the trolleybuses. (PJ Thompson)

55.   Northwards from Denton, the route passed into Audenshaw and Guide Bridge. In Guide Lane, trolleybuses crossed over the electrified Manchester to Sheffield railway at Guide Bridge station, where Manchester BUT 1334 is seen as it approaches Guide Bridge from the Denton direction.

56. At Guide Bridge, the Haughton Green trolleybuses met those on service 219. Here, Manchester BUT 1304 is seen turning into Guide Lane at the Guide Bridge turning circle. Note the conductor pulling the handle to set the frog. Compare this view with that seen previously at this point (photograph 35). 26th March 1959. (RB Parr)

F 9192

A.G.P.T.D

8D

DAILY
WORKMAN
RETURN

Mon.

Tues.

Wed.

Thurs.

Fri.

Sat.

Sun.

This Ticket is issued subject to
regulations up to 8.0 a.m.
Is available for day of issue
only between the points stated.

FROM GREY MARE LANE

FROM STALYBRIDGE

Bell Punch Company, London. B4476

GEE CROSS AND HYDE

57.   Gee Cross terminus, the southernmost on the system, was in Cheshire, nine miles from Piccadilly. It was situated at the junction of Dowson Road and Stockport Road, where there was a large turning circle of wiring. Post war Crossley trolleybuses 1214 (left, at the terminal stop) and 1233 are seen here. (J Fozard)

58.   Shortly after leaving the terminus, the route passed through Gee Cross village where Crossley 1208 is seen en route to Piccadilly on 5th August 1962. Note the white 'o' on the offside lower corner panel – this denoted 'overhead', a warning to any following trolleybus driver that overtaking this bus was not recommended! (PJ Thompson)

59.   A quiet moment at Hyde Market Place is seen here, showing Crossley 1214 en route for Gee Cross. There was a short working facility at Hyde, a short distance south of the Market Place, where a loop of wiring ran around Smithy Lane and Lumn Road. In addition, adjacent to the Market Place, another wiring loop was erected by SHMD, but this was never connected to the main route wires, and it was consequently unused. (J Fozard)

➜ 60. At Denton, there was a major wiring junction at Crown Point. This has already been discussed in part under the Haughton Green section. The short working service 210X turned here from Piccadilly, which was the usual haunt of the post war Crossley 6-wheelers. The turn-back loop was via Inman Street and Saxon Street. Seen here at Saxon Street on 15th September 1951 is brand new 6-wheeler 1254. At this date it was the newest trolleybus in the fleet, the final ones of the batch, 1252 and 1255, not entering service until October. (IA Yearsley)

➜   61. At Thornley Park, situated on the Denton UDC / Manchester (Gorton) boundary, there was a turn-back loop at the wide junction of Hyde Road and Kingsdale Road. This was not nearly as well used as the Denton turn back, but it did see intensive use during the Suez crisis in late 1956 / early 1957, when a temporary trolleybus service was operated to here, partly replacing motorbus services. Crossley 6-wheeler 1254, seen in the previous photograph and now eleven years old, is passing the turning loop on a journey from Denton to Piccadilly.
23rd June 1962. (PJ Thompson)

← 62. Gorton Baths was the location of another turning loop which allowed turns from either the Piccadilly or Hyde directions. Its main purpose was to accommodate the many extra journeys that ran to cater for visitors to the popular Belle Vue pleasure gardens a short distance nearer to the city centre, and also for works journeys. This was the furthest point from the city on the Hyde Road route that pre-war trolleybuses normally ever worked in service and Leyland 6-wheeler 1065 is seen here on the loop at Johnson Street. (R Marshall)

← 63. The Belle Vue pleasure gardens site was located on the south side of Hyde Road at Gorton. Dubbed 'The Gateway to a Thousand Pleasures', it comprised a zoo, gardens and amusement centre, as well as many other amenities such as a speedway stadium and exhibition hall. This evocative scene at the stop outside the main entrance shows Crossley 1227 en route for Piccadilly. On the left is the queue of expectant patrons waiting to enter the site.
(J Copland / P Watson)

64.   Further west along Hyde Road, at West Gorton, trolleybuses passed under the main railway to London at the 'Fenians' Arch'. The name commemorates a notorious incident here in 1867. As part of the railway electrification scheme in the late 1950s, the arch was replaced by this modern bridge, under which Crossley 1213 is passing on 1st July 1962.
(PJ Thompson)

HYDE ROAD
GARAGE

65.   This glimpse into the garage dates from the early 1950s, when 58 trolleybuses were based here, including several early wartime Crossley vehicles. From the left are 1147, 1158 and 1146. Note that 1147 bears the destination 'Hyde Rd Depot' – an unusual display for a Manchester trolleybus. Both depots were normally referred to as 'garage'.
(GMTS Via PJ Thompson)

➜   66. Hyde Road garage was one of two garages which housed trolleybuses, and from 1956 it had responsibility for the whole fleet. The Transport Department workshops were also located here, where major overhauls and rebuilds took place. In tram days new trams were constructed here, including the famous 'Pullman' or 'Pilcher' cars built in the early 1930s. By the early 1960s extensive rebuilding work was in progress, which would remove the distinctive arched doorways. In this view, BUT 1354 is emerging from the garage to take up service at Stevenson Square. To reach this point, it will run via Devonshire Street North, Chancellor Lane, Pin Mill Brow and Great Ancoats Street. At the time of this photograph, much of this wiring was no longer used by service trolleybuses. (J Fozard)

GREENHEYS

67.   Greenheys terminus was in Platt Lane, Fallowfield. Trolleybuses turned on a one way loop from Lloyd Street South, via Hart Road and Platt Lane, then turned back into Lloyd Street South. Crossley 1157 is seen at the terminal stop on a quiet, sunny day, 18th June 1955. (R Dunning)

68.　　Having just started its journey back to Corporation Street, post-war Crossley 1212 is seen turning from Platt Lane into Lloyd Street South in the early 1950s. The vehicle is displaying the original service number '30', which was replaced by '213' in 1952. Note the disused tram track in the foreground. (N R Knight)

69.　　At the south end of Lloyd Street South, there was a long siding in the wiring. This was to accommodate football specials to the nearby Maine Road ground of Manchester City AFC. BUT 1330 is seen here on 3rd April 1959. (PJ Thompson)

70.   At the other end of Lloyd Street South, inbound and outbound trolleybuses ran in different streets. Inbound vehicles ran via Monton Street and Carter Street, whilst Greenheys bound vehicles ran via Lloyd Street North. At the southern end of this arrangement there was a wiring link to allow trolleybuses to turn here, this point being known as 'Moss Lane East'. This view is of the northern end, and shows BUT 1347 about to turn from Burlington Street into Lloyd Street North on a journey to Greenheys. In the left foreground the inbound wires coming from Carter Street are evident. 31st May 1959. (PJ Thompson)

71.   Between Burlington Street and Brunswick Street, trolleybuses ran for a short distance along Oxford Road beside the Manchester University Library building. Here, BUT 1361 is seen turning from Brunswick Street into Oxford Road, and the wires turning into Burlington Street can be seen in the background. The Library building is on the right of this view taken on 31st May 1959, the last day of trolleybus operation on the route. In Brunswick Street, near this point, there was a short working turn back loop around side streets. Vehicles showed '213X University' when terminating here. This was the terminus of the service until 1946, when the extension to Moss Lane East and Platt Lane was opened. (PJ Thompson)

72.　　At Ardwick Green, the service 213 wires crossed those of service 210 to Hyde, as it passed from Brunswick Street into Higher Ardwick. Hyde Road, with the clock tower of Hyde Road garage evident, is in the background, as BUT 1347 turns into Brunswick Street on the final day of 213 operation. (PJ Thompson)

73.　　At the northern end of Chancellor Lane, there was a major wiring junction where the 213 trolleybuses met the Ashton Old Road route as they crossed Fairfield Street towards Pin Mill Brow. There were wiring connections here to allow vehicles on the Ashton Old Road services to run to and from Hyde Road garage from the Audenshaw direction. BUT 1340 on service 213 crosses from Pin Mill Brow into Chancellor Lane at this point on 3rd April 1959 underneath the crossings of the wiring layout. (PJ Thompson)

MOSTON

74.   In 1941, the Moston service wires were extended one third of a mile from The Gardeners Arms, along Greengate to the AV Roe aircraft factory, where components for the famous Lancaster bomber were made. The terminus was in the special bus station which served this strategic site.   Trolleybuses running to here always showed 'Greengate' rather than being more specific as to the actual terminus. Crossley 1176, the last of the pre-war trolleybuses (but which did not enter service until 1943), is seen at the AV Roe terminus during an enthusiasts' tour, hence the deserted site. It should be noted that all Manchester's trolleybuses delivered in wartime between 1940 and 1943 were built to full peacetime standards. (DF Parker)

Oc 1485

Outward	A. C. P. T.	Inward
1		8
2	1d	7
3		6
4		5
5		4
6		3
7		2
8		1
Dog		Parcel

This Ticket must be produced or given up on demand, and is issued subject to the Bye-laws and Regulations of the Corporation

Williamson, Printer, Ashton

← 75. This is a glimpse of the Greengate terminus, as it normally looked at shift change time just after the war. It demonstrates how factory workers used to rely almost entirely on public transport. The row of trolley booms in the background shows where the trolleybuses loaded. This view was taken from the first floor of the AVRO offices. (Manchester Corporation Transport via M Eyre)

← 76. Leyland 1113 leans over as it turns round at the Gardeners Arms terminus of services 211 and 212. The wires off to the right are in Greengate, and lead to the AV Roe factory. (NR Knight)

77. This is the Gardeners Arms terminal stop, outside the Gardeners Arms itself on 19th April 1955. Two Leylands are seen, 1108 and 1102. Note that both vehicles retain the slip board brackets below the front destination indicators. This was an original feature of the vehicles numbered in the 1100 series, and also the post war four wheel Crossleys. It is doubtful whether the slip boards were ever displayed. On the right, the guard of 1108 is carrying his traditional enamel tea can. (R Dunning)

78.　　South of the Gardeners Arms, at the junction with Moston Lane and Nuthurst Road, there was a short working turning circle which was not frequently used in post war days. Seen passing this point in June 1955 is brand new BUT 1302. This vehicle was the first of the batch to be delivered, and it was initially used on the 211 Moston service. It was soon removed from the area due to adverse criticism from local residents, who had to endure the life expired pre-war trolleybuses and knew that the comfortable new trolleybuses would not be their replacement. Behind 1302 is Crossley 1021, one of the rather jaded pre-war vehicles which would soon be replaced by a motorbus.

← 79. This scene is in Moston Lane at Bacup Brow Farm near Nuthurst Road. One of the pre-war Leyland TB4 vehicles, 1034, is seen city bound on service 212 running along the concrete road surface. The date is 24th April 1955, the last day of trolleybus operation on the 212 service. Note that 1034 is displaying 'High St' and not 'Church St', this being an alternative description for the city centre terminus which was used on the original destination blinds. (R Dunning)

80.   At the 'Ben Brierley' (a hostelry named after a local poet), there was a trolleybus junction where the 211 and 212 services diverged to run into the city centre via Oldham Road and Rochdale Road respectively. There was also a large turning loop here used by services 211X and the much more frequent 212X. Crossley 1144 is seen at the terminal loop on service 212X on Sunday 3rd October 1954, showing 'Football Match', a display used by specials to the Manchester City Maine Road ground near Platt Lane. (R Dunning)

81. From the 'Ben Brierley', service 211 trolleybuses ran via Kenyon Lane, Lightbowne Road and Thorp Road to Newton Heath, where they turned into Oldham Road to travel into the city centre. Crossley 1025, with plain fleet number, is seen at Thorpe Road and is about to make the turn into Oldham Road. (NR Knight)

→ 82. The 212 service ran further westwards along Moston Lane and turned sharp left into Upper Conran Street towards Rochdale Road. At this point there was a three way wiring junction, where the peak hour only 214 circular service diverged. This service was unusual in that it operated in an anti-clockwise direction only in the morning peak, and a clockwise direction in the evening peak. The tightness of the turns here was one of the reasons why six-wheel trolleybuses were not used on the Moston services. A pre-war Leyland trolleybus, 1028, is seen making the turn into Upper Conran Street. On the left, the 214 wires turn into Moston Lane. Note the round mirror fixed to the traction pole on the left of this view. This was provided by the Transport Department to allow trolleybus drivers to see around the corner. (NR Knight)

→ 83. Near Queens Park, Harpurhey, service 212 trolleybuses joined Rochdale Road to run into the city centre. Crossley 1167 is at Sudbury Street heading towards the city on a service from the 'Ben Brierley' on the last day of operation, Sunday, 24th April 1955. In the far left background, beyond the church, is the Conran Street / Rochdale Road junction, where services 212 and 214 diverged. (R Dunning)

ROCHDALE ROAD
GARAGE

84.   The Rochdale Road trolleybus garage was purpose built for the first Manchester trolleybuses, and had a capacity of 115 vehicles. It lay on the south side of Rochdale Road. Inside there were ten parking 'roads' lettered A to J. This interior view, taken about six months after operations commenced, shows a selection of almost new trolleybuses, and reveals how the rear of these vehicles originally looked, with streamlined livery, full destination display, and a prominent 'Manchester Corporation' legend on the lower rear panel. In view, from the left, are Crossley 4 wheelers 1021, 1024, 1001, 1000 and 1011. (GMTS)

85.　Crossley 1027, seen here with substantial accident damage, was one of Rochdale Road garage's allocation of vehicles. Of interest is the destination display, which shows the original route number '36' for the Gardeners Arms via Oldham Road service introduced in 1941. This was renumbered to 31 in 1948, and then to 211 in 1953. Rochdale Road garage lost its trolleybuses in April 1956, when those remaining were transferred to Hyde Road garage.

MANCHESTER CITY CENTRE

86.　The Church Street terminal was dominated by tall, soot stained offices and warehouses. Loops in the wiring were provided to allow vehicles on service 212 and 212X to overtake each other. Leyland 1130 stands here before departing for the Gardeners Arms. The outward route to Rochdale Road was via Oldham Street, New Cross and Swan Street.

87.   The 213 service from Greenheys terminated at Corporation Street. Inbound trolleybuses reached here from Great Ancoats Street via Swan Street and Miller Street, returning via a route traversing Mayes Street, Redfern Street, Swan Street, Rochdale Road, Thompson Street, and Oldham Road. It was not until July 1948 that the service was extended from Thompson Street to this point, which was near the Victoria and Exchange railway stations. In this busy scene at the terminal stop, Crossley 1145 stands in front of a post-war Crossley six-wheeler, both types being commonly used on the service in the mid 1950s. (C Carter)

88.   Services using Stevenson Square were the 211 (Oldham Road) and the 215/216 (Ashton New Road) services. Inbound trolleybuses ran via Newton Street, where BUT 1306, arriving from Audenshaw, is seen making the turn into Hilton Street which led to the Square. The wiring in the opposite direction, not used by vehicles in service, gave a connection from Piccadilly to Great Ancoats Street, and to Rochdale Road garage. (J Fozard)

89. Stevenson Square is situated between Newton Street and Oldham Street, and lies parallel to Piccadilly. Hilton Street runs through the Square and Lever Street crosses it. This view dates from the latter half of 1938, just after trolleybuses were introduced and shows the original arrangement for trolleybuses before the Moston services were introduced. The rear of Leyland 6-wheeler 1080 is evident, working on the 27 service to Audenshaw (The Snipe). Note the tram wires in Lever Street in the upper foreground, and also alongside the trolleybus wires in the Square itself. (Manchester Libraries)

90. This busy scene in Stevenson Square dates from the mid 1950s, just prior to the closure of the 211 Oldham Road service and before the BUT vehicles were introduced. In the foreground are two trolleybuses that have just arrived from Ashton New Road. Crossley 1021 is on service 215X to Edge Lane and behind this is Leyland 1129 on service 216 to Stalybridge. Leyland 1110 is in the left background on the 211X service to the 'Ben Brierley'. (C Carter)

91. The original pre-war fleet was fast disappearing by the time of this photograph dated 29th September 1955. In this view, Crossley 1001 is waiting to move onto the 215 / 216 stand at Stevenson Square before departing for Stalybridge. The Moston route had closed the previous month, and the new BUT trolleybuses were entering service. 1001 would be withdrawn at the beginning of 1956. When it was new in 1938, this vehicle was used to test an experimental method of current collection using one trolley pole.
(J Copland / P Watson)

92. The new regime of BUT trolleybuses in Stevenson Square is shown here. 1320 is working on a 215X journey to Edge Lane, with 1313 behind on a 216X working to Ashton. The loading stand for the 215 / 216 is on the right. (J Fozard)

93.   Ashton vehicles were rarely seen in Stevenson Square and such appearances were usually as a result of a defective Manchester vehicle being exchanged in Ashton. On this occasion in July 1964, Ashton Crossley 80 is visiting on an enthusiasts' tour. It is using the loop wiring, formerly used as the Moston service terminus, which was retained after that service was withdrawn. Manchester BUT 1337 slips in behind on the 215 service. At this time, Ashton 80 was the sole survivor in service of either Ashton's or Manchester's postwar Crossley trolleybuses, and it ran until October 1964. (JS King)

---

(72) Starting
   To move the bus forward, place the hand lever in the "trolley forward" position and depress the power pedal (left foot) on to the first notch and then release the hand brake.
   A slow and steady depression of the power pedal will give uniform acceleration without jerks. Do not attempt to find each notch in turn. When starting on a gradient, depress the pedal more slowly to avoid tripping the circuit breakers. First or second notch will need to be engaged before the hand brake can be released.

94.   Trolleybuses left Stevenson Square by way of Oldham Street, where, until the mid 1950s, there was a parallel set of wires used by service 212 trolleybuses coming from their Church Street terminus. At New Cross, Ashton New Road trolleybuses turned right into Great Ancoats Street, a manoeuvre that BUT 1302 is about to make. (DF Parker)

95.   The Hyde Road trolleybuses terminated at the north west side of Piccadilly Gardens at George Street. This typical scene shows Crossley 1226 here in the summer of 1953. There are Coronation decorations evident on the left, as well as a green Salford City Transport Daimler motor bus. (J Copland / P Watson)

96.   At the other end of Piccadilly Gardens, in Portland Street, was the terminal for the Ashton Old Road services. Trolleybuses reached here from Fairfield Street via Aytoun Street. In this mid 1950s view, new BUT 1352 is about to make the turn from Aytoun Street into Portland Street. Behind is postwar Crossley 6 wheeler 1245 working a peak hour journey from Ashton Old Road. Note that the destination on 1352 is 'Audenshaw The Snipe'. (J Fozard)

→ 97. Pre-war Crossley 1018 is seen pulling on to the terminal stand at Portland Street. Behind it is a Hyde Road service trolleybus, which has come from George Street via the Piccadilly bus station on the west side of Piccadilly Gardens. It will then pass the Ashton Old Road trolleybus stands using by-pass wiring. In late 1956 the Hyde Road trolleybuses were re-routed away from George Street to terminate on the opposite side of Portland Street. (J Fozard)

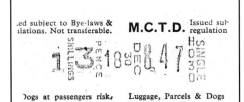

→   98. In postwar years, up to the arrival of the BUT trolleybuses, the pre-war 6 wheelers operated peak hour journeys along both Ashton Old and New Roads, as well as the Greenheys service. This one is Crossley 1059, seen with poles down in Portland Street in the late 1940s, its blinds set for a 29X journey to Audenshaw Road 'The Trough'. Note that the rear destination display has been reduced to show only a service number and final destination, and also the less extensive streamlined livery which applied immediately after the war. (J Fozard)

99.   Seen waiting at the main stand at Portland Street is pre-war Ashton 6-wheeler 47. This vehicle was one of a pair purchased in 1938 for the Manchester service. Note the prominent sign on the shelter to the right of this late 1940s view. (WJ Haynes)

→   100. Ashton and Manchester vehicles stand together in Portland Street beside Piccadilly Gardens, showing the intricate wiring layout which allowed full flexibility, including the through wiring for the Hyde Road trolleybuses. Ashton wartime Sunbeam W 63, rebodied by Bond in 1955, is seen waiting to depart for Stalybridge, in front of a Manchester postwar Crossley.

→   101.   In mid 1957, the introduction of a one way traffic scheme in Portland Street resulted in the Ashton Old Road terminus being moved across the road to where the Hyde Road trolleybuses had been terminating since the previous December. This meant that the terminal was approached via London Road, where Ashton wartime Sunbeam 62 with 1958 Roe body is seen near Whitworth Street, followed by Manchester BUT 1304. The front blind on 62 has already been changed in readiness for its return journey. Today, this location is where the Metrolink trams cross London Road to enter their undercroft terminus at Piccadilly station.
5th May 1964 (PJ Thompson)

102.   This BUT (1343) is seen crossing into Portland Street from Newton Street, having come from Hyde Road garage to take up service at Portland Street. From May 1965, the direct wiring from the garage via Downing Street and London Road was removed due to construction of the Mancunian Way. This meant that journeys from the garage to Piccadilly then had to run via Pin Mill Brow, Great Ancoats Street and Newton Street. Returning to the garage from Piccadilly involved running to the Grey Mare Lane loop to turn, then using the left turn connection from Ashton Old Road into Chancellor Lane. 14th August 1965 (RDH Symons)

→   103. Manchester BUT 1337 comes round the corner into Portland Street at the end of a journey from Stalybridge. In the left background is the Piccadilly head office of Manchester Corporation Transport Department. In 1963 this was moved to Devonshire Street North on the Hyde Road garage site. (J Fozard)

→   104.   The wiring in Portland Street was complex, with separate loops for each service. This is Ashton BUT 83 on the 219 service stand, although it appears that it has arrived using the through wiring, and the driver is about to transfer the trolley booms to the loop. This view was taken on the last day of 219 trolleybus operation, 10th October 1964. (PJ Thompson)

105.   One of the pair of 1940 built Ashton Crossleys that remained in service after 1956 is seen at the 219 stand in Portland Street on 18th February 1958. By this time they were not normally used in all day service, and 54 is probably working a peak hour extra journey. (PJ Thompson)

106.   Trolleybuses in varied liveries are lined up in Portland Street. On the left, Manchester BUT 1324 is pulling away from the 219 stand, and is about to overtake an Ashton BUT and Manchester 1331, newly repainted in the simplified livery which applied from 1959 onwards.
(V Nutton / Travel Lens Photographic)

107.   Rebodied Ashton wartime Sunbeam 62 waits at the 218 stand in Portland Street before departing for Stalybridge. The intricate loop wiring can be seen. (JS King)

108. Many of the Manchester Crossleys delivered in early wartime survived to use the new wiring arrangements at Portland Street. This view dated 14th June 1958 shows 1158 working on a peak hour 212X journey terminating in Aytoun Street, and passing Crossley 6 wheeler 1255 at the Hyde Road stop. (CW Routh)

➔ 109. In December 1956, the George Street terminus of the Hyde 210 service was moved to this location, seven months in advance of the similar change to the terminus of the Ashton Old Road services. The 210 stop was near the junction with Aytoun Street. Here, Ashton BUT 84, immediately prior to turning into Aytoun Street, overtakes Manchester Crossley 1233 waiting to depart for Gee Cross. Both these vehicles will end their journeys in Cheshire. (CW Routh)

➔ 110. Hyde Road trolleybuses turned from Aytoun Street into Whitworth Street, from where they reached London Road. Ashton Old Road trolleybuses went forward into Fairfield Street, crossing London Road. The wiring here allowed trolleybuses to turn at Whitworth Street instead of Portland Street and peak hour vehicles terminating here showed 'London Road'. This scene shows Crossley 1201 making the turn from Aytoun Street into Whitworth Street, negotiating the automatic frog. (AE Jones)

Fleet details

Oldham

Fleet nos	Reg nos	Type	Chassis	Body	Year new	Out of service
1, 2	BU 3861 / 54	2-axle	Railless	Short	1925	1926

Ashton

Fleet nos	Reg nos	Type	Chassis	Body	Year new	Out of service
50-57	See below	2-axle	Railless	Short	1925	1937-9
49	CTD 787	2-axle	Crossley	Crossley	1937	1956
48, 52, 55	CTD 547-49	2-axle	Leyland	English .Electric	1937	1956
58	CNE 474	3-axle	Crossley	Crossley	1938	1955
46,47	CTF 313-14	3-axle	Crossley	Crossley	1938	1951
50,51,53, 54,56,57, 59,60	ETE 811-18	2-axle	Crossley	Crossley	1940	1954-1960
61-64	FTE 645-48	2-axle	Sunbeam	Park Royal	1944	1963-5
65-66	FTJ 401-400	2-axle	Sunbeam	Roe	1946	1960
77-81	LTC 771-75	2-axle	Crossley	Crossley	1950	1963-4
82-89	YTE 821-28	2-axle	BUT	Bond	1956	1966

Notes

50-7 Registrations :- TD 2362, 2497, 3147, 3148, 3207, 3208, 3262, 3344.

49, 58 Built in 1936 and originally Crossley demonstration vehicles

61-64 Rebodied by Bond in 1955/4 (63, 64) and Roe in 1958 (61, 62)

Manchester

Fleet nos	Reg nos	Type	Chassis	Body	Year new	Out of service
1000-27	DXJ 951-978	2 axle	Crossley	Crossley	1938	1953-6
1028-37	DXJ 979-988	2 axle	Leyland	Crossley	1938	1951-5
1050-61	DXJ 989-993 ENB175-181	3 axle	Crossley	Crossley	1938	1950-6
1062-87	ENB182-207	3-axle	Leyland	Crossley	1938	1950-6
1100-36	GNA 18-54	2-axle	Leyland/	English Electric	1940-1	1954-9
1137-76	GNA 55-94	2-axle	Crossley	Crossley	1940-3	1953-1960
1200-37	JVU 707-44	2-axle	Crossley	Crossley	1949-50	1963
1240-55	JVU 745-60	3-axle	Crossley	Crossley	1951	1963
1301-62	ONE701-62	2-axle	BUT	Burlingham	1955-6	1962-6

Note The pre-war and wartime Crossley bodies were built using Metro-Cammell frames.

ROLLING STOCK

Readers will note that the majority of views in this section are of Ashton vehicles. This reflects the highly standardised nature of the large Manchester fleet, whereas that of Ashton, although numerically much smaller, had a greater variety of types, including some 'one-off' vehicles.

111.   Crossley's prototype 6-wheel trolleybus, type TDD6, was built in 1936 and was tested on Ashton's Hathershaw route. Built primarily to attract orders from London Transport, it was very much to London specification. It was purchased by Ashton in 1938 and numbered 58, Seen here in the mid-1940s at Ashton Market Place, it had a prominent service number display under the destination indicator which was later blanked off completely. No 58 was withdrawn in 1955. (WJ Haynes)

112.   The other Crossley trolleybus prototype, a 4-wheeler type TDD4, was also built in 1936. It became Ashton 49 in 1937 after being tested on the Hathershaw route running in Crossley Motors' green and cream livery (see photograph 4). This early 1950s view shows that the original 3 piece Manchester style destination indicators had been considerably reduced, giving the vehicle a rather odd frontal appearance. It was later rebuilt with a standard Ashton destination and number display and survived in service until 1956. (C Carter)

113.   In 1937, Ashton purchased three Leyland TB4 vehicles with English Electric bodywork numbered 48, 52 and 55. Initially, before the routes to Manchester were opened, they were used on the Hathershaw route (fitted with trolley wheels), replacing some of the Railless vehicles. This one, as seen here, was rebuilt with an enlarged destination indicator and a separate route number display. 55 waits to depart from Ashton Market Place on the 217 Haughton Green service. (C Carter)

GUIDE BRIDGE

29

ASHTON OLD R^d
OPENSHAW

1000

DXJ·951

114.   Manchester's pre-war trolleybus fleet all had the same general appearance although the 6-wheelers were obviously longer.   Most had Crossley bodies built on Metro-Cammell frames, the only exceptions being the 37 Leylands delivered in the early years of the war whose bodies were by English Electric. Ashton had two 6-wheelers and eight 4-wheelers with Crossley bodies to the same general design. This is 1000, numerically Manchester's first trolleybus, which is seen in the doorway of Rochdale Road garage. Note the destination display is set for service 29 to Guide Bridge, the terminus of this service until March 1940 when it was extended into Ashton. (Manchester Libraries)

115.   Four wartime Sunbeam W trolleybuses, with Park Royal 'utility' bodies, were delivered to Ashton in 1944 and numbered 61 to 64. All these were rebodied in the 1950s, 63 and 64 with Bond bodies in 1955 and 1954 respectively and the remaining two with Roe bodies in 1958. When rebodied, 64 was the first Ashton trolleybus to have the new peacock blue livery, although its original red centre band was replaced by cream before the vehicle returned to service. This is 63 at Ashton Market Place in its original 'utility' form with a small destination indicator. (R Marshall)

← 116. Two additional 'utility' Sunbeam trolleybuses were added in 1946. Numbered 65 and 66, these had Roe bodies and ran unaltered, except for the revised livery, until 1960. They were sold to Bradford City Transport, who intended to fit the chassis with forward entrance East Lancashire Coachbuilders bodies, and number them 821 and 820 respectively in the fleet. Sadly this never happened and the vehicles were subsequently scrapped. 65 is seen here on 22nd October 1960, at Bradford's Thornbury works, in the condition that it latterly ran in Ashton.

117.   Both Ashton's and Manchester's first post war Crossley trolleybuses were eight feet wide vehicles, the first trolleybuses of this width in either fleet. The 4-wheelers were designated 'Empire', and of the 45 vehicles of this type built, 38 went to Manchester and 5 to Ashton. The remaining two chassis were delivered to Cleethorpes Corporation and fitted with Roe bodies. This view in Bow Street, Ashton, gives a direct comparison between the Manchester and Ashton vehicles. The Ashton examples were the first in that fleet to have a service number display from new (apart from the Crossley prototype 6-wheeler of 1936). 77, the first of the batch, is in full dark blue and red livery, and displays the service number 28, which by the time of this view (October 1950) had been discontinued and was officially service 218. The Manchester vehicle, 1212, displays the new number 219. All these vehicles were withdrawn in 1963, except for Ashton 80 which lasted until October 1964.
(AT Smith / AB Cross)

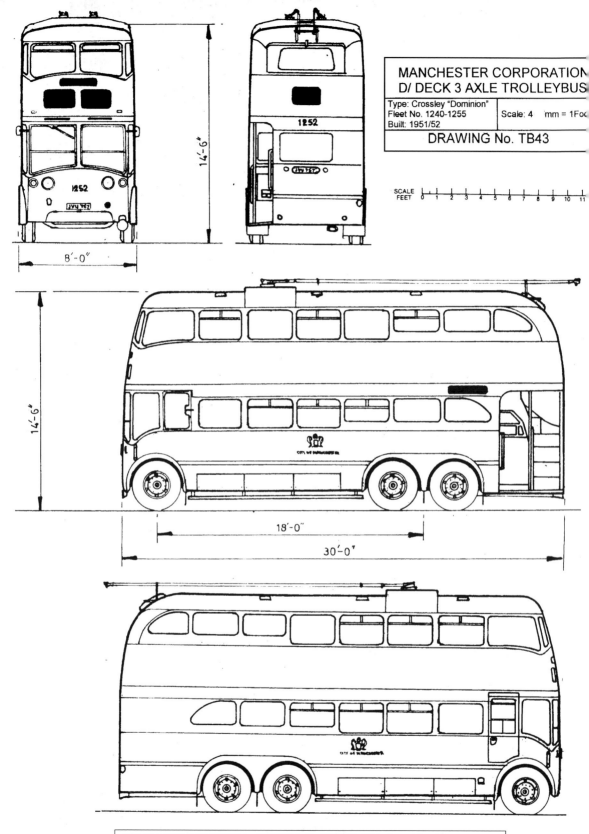

MANCHESTER CORPORATION
D/ DECK 3 AXLE TROLLEYBUS

Type: Crossley "Dominion"
Fleet No. 1240-1255
Built: 1951/52

Scale: 4 mm = 1Foot

DRAWING No. TB43

SCALE
FEET 0 1 2 3 4 5 6 7 8 9 10 11

14'-6"

8'-0"

1252

14'-6"

18'-0"

30'-0"

118.　Manchester's 16 postwar 6- wheel Crossleys, delivered in 1951, were given the type name 'Dominion', and these were the only examples built.　They spent their entire life on the peak hour and Saturdays 210X service to Denton, as well as other peak hour workings along Ashton Old and New Roads, and to Greenheys.　Union resistance denied their more widespread use, not helped by initial problems with very heavy steering.　All were withdrawn in 1963, and no 1250 was secured for preservation and is now on display at the Greater Manchester Museum of Transport.　In this view, 'Dominion' 1246 is seen in George Street, Piccadilly on 1st April 1956, with a contemporary Crossley 'Empire' 4-wheeler behind it. (AD Packer)

119.　The final delivery of 70 trolleybuses came in the mid 1950s. These had unique BUT 9612T chassis assembled locally at the Crossley factory at Errwood Park, Stockport.　Manchester's 62 vehicles had Burlingham bodies built in Blackpool, whilst Ashton's eight had Bond bodies built at Wythenshawe, Manchester.　Given the fleet numbers 1301 to 1362, the Manchester batch entered service from June 1955 until March 1956 (see photograph 78), whilst Ashton 82 to 89 came later in September and October of 1956. Most of these fine vehicles lasted until the end of trolleybus operation in December 1966. The Ashton vehicles, whose bodies were the last bus bodies built by Bond, were particularly handsome, as this view of 83 at Guide Bridge in September 1963 shows. It has just turned at the circle here from the Ashton direction, and is waiting to return to Ashton. The conductor, equipped with an 'Ultimate' ticket machine, is probably about to assist the driver in setting the destination blind. (PJ Thompson)

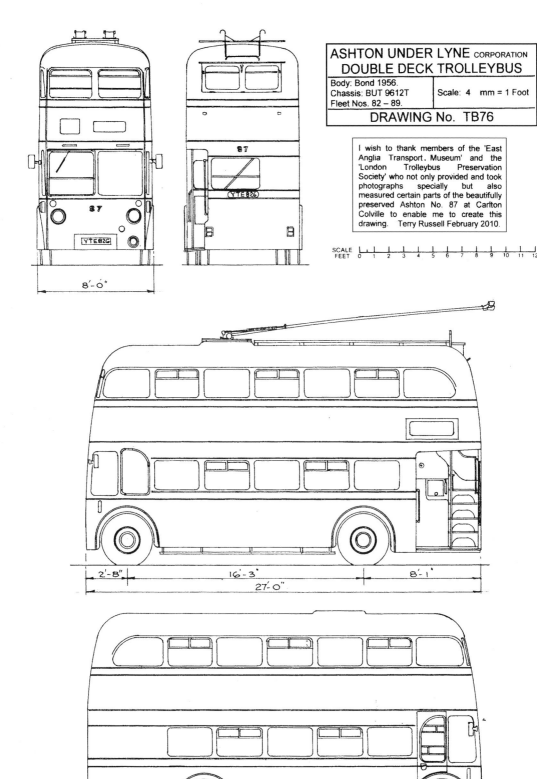

ASHTON UNDER LYNE CORPORATION
DOUBLE DECK TROLLEYBUS

Body: Bond 1956. Chassis: BUT 9612T Fleet Nos. 82 – 89.	Scale: 4 mm = 1 Foot

DRAWING No. TB76

I wish to thank members of the 'East Anglia Transport. Museum' and the 'London Trolleybus Preservation Society' who not only provided and took photographs specially but also measured certain parts of the beautifully preserved Ashton No. 87 at Carlton Colville to enable me to create this drawing.   Terry Russell February 2010.

SCALE
FEET 0 1 2 3 4 5 6 7 8 9 10 11 12

8'-0"

87

YTE82G

87

YTE82G

2'-8"   16'-3"   8'-1"
27'-0"

DRAWN BY:—TERRY RUSSELL, "CHACESIDE", ST. LEONARDS PARK, HORSHAM, W.SUSSEX. RH13 6EG
SEND 4 FIRST CLASS STAMPS FOR COMPLETE LIST OF PUBLIC TRANSPORT DRAWINGS

FINALE

120.   Although trolleybuses ran in public service for the last time on 30th December 1966 (see Historical background), two enthusiasts' tours were allowed on the following day, but only using Manchester's wiring. Both tours used privately preserved vehicles, these being Rotherham 6-wheel Daimler 44 and Manchester 1344, which had last operated in 1964, having been one of the first BUT vehicles to be withdrawn. The pair are seen together in Ashton Old Road at Fairfield Wells near Ashbrook Street. (RDH Symons)

Stevenson Square	Piccadilly	**Manchester's Last Trolleybus**
		Issued to Commemorate the End of TROLLEYBUS OPERATION
		Saturday, 31st December, 1966
		Souvenir Ticket Presented by Manchester Transport Historical Society

TRAMWAY CLASSICS   Robert J Harley

Aldgate & Stepney Tramways to Hackney and West India Docks
Barnet & Finchley Tramways to Golders Green and Highgate
Bath Tramways   Peter Davey and Paul Welland
Blackpool Tramways 1933-66 75 years of Streamliners   Stephen Lockwood
Bournemouth & Poole Tramways Roy C Anderson
Bristol's Tramways A massive system radiating to ten destinations Peter Davey
Burton & Ashby Tramways An often rural light railway Peter M White
Camberwell & West Norwood Trys including Herne Hill and Peckham Rye
Chester Tramways Barry M Marsden
Chesterfield Tramways a typical provincial system Barry Marsden
Clapham & Streatham Tramways including Tooting and Earlsfield J.Gent & J.Meredith
Derby Tramways a comprehensive city system Colin Barker
Dover's Tramways to River and Maxton
East Ham & West Ham Trys from Stratford and Ilford down to the docks
Edgware & Willesden Tramways including Sudbury, Paddington & Acton
Embankment & Waterloo Trys including the fondly remembered Kingsway Subway
Exeter & Taunton Tramways Two charming small systems J B Perkin
Fulwell - Home for Trams, Trolleys and Buses Professor Bryan Woodriff
Gosport & Horndean Tramways Martin Petch
Great Yarmouth Tramways A seaside pleasure trip Dave Mackley
Hammersmith & Hounslow Trys branches to Hanwell, Acton & Shepherds Bush
Hampstead & Highgate Trys from Tottenham Court Road and King's Cross Dave Jones
Hastings Tramways A sea front and rural ride
Holborn & Finsbury Trys Angel-Balls Pond Road - Moorgate - Bloomsbury
Huddersfield Tramways the original municipal system Stephen Lockwood
Hull Tramways Level crossings and bridges abound Paul Morfitt & Malcolm Wells
Ilford & Barking Tramways to Barkingside, Chadwell Heath and Beckton
Ilkeston & Glossop Tramways Barry M Marsden
Ipswich Tramways   Colin Barker
Keighley Tramways & Trolleybuses Barry M Marsden
Kingston & Wimbledon Trys incl Hampton Court, Tooting & four routes from Kingston
Liverpool Tramways - 1 Eastern Routes
Liverpool Tramways - 2 Southern Routes
Liverpool Tramways - 3 Northern Routes A trilogy by Brian Martin
Llandudno & Colwyn Bay Tramways Stephen Lockwood
Maidstone & Chatham Trys from Barming to Loose and from Strood to Rainham
Margate & Ramsgate Tramways including Broadstairs
North Kent Tramways including Bexley, Erith, Dartford, Gravesend and Sheerness
Norwich Tramways A popular system comprising ten main routes David Mackley
Nottinghamshire & Derbyshire Try including the Matlock Cable Tramway Barry M Marsden
Portsmouth Tramways including Southsea Martin Petch
Reading Tramways Three routes - a comprehensive coverage Edgar Jordon
Scarborough Tramway including the Scarborough Cliff Lifts Barry M Marsden
Seaton & Eastbourne Tramways Attractive miniature lines
Shepherds Bush & Uxbridge Tramways including Ealing John C Gillham
South London Tramways 1903-33 Wandsworth - Dartford
South London Tramways 1933-52 The Thames to Croydon
Southampton Tramways Martin Petch

Southend-on-Sea Tramways including the Pier Electric Railway
Southwark & Deptford Tramways including the Old Kent Road
Stamford Hill Tramways including Stoke Newington and Liverpool Street
Twickenham & Kingston Trys extending to Richmond Bridge and Wimbledon
Victoria & Lambeth Tramways to Nine Elms, Brixton and Kennington
Waltham Cross & Edmonton Trys to Finsbury Park, Wood Green and Enfield
Walthamstow & Leyton Trys including Clapton, Chingford Hill and Woodford
Wandsworth & Battersea Trys from Hammersmith, Putney and Chelsea
York Tramways & Trolleybuses Barry M Marsden

Tramways included in the Trolleybuses series -
see Darlington Trolleybuses

TROLLEYBUSES

Birmingham Trolleybuses ... David Harvey
Bournemouth Trolleybuses ... Malcolm N Pearce
Bradford Trolleybuses ... Stephen Lockwood
Brighton Trolleybuses ... Andrew Henbest
Cardiff Trolleybuses ... Stephen Lockwood
Chesterfield Trolleybuses ... Barry M Marsden
Croydon Trolleybuses ... Terry Russell
Darlington Trolleybuses ... Stephen Lockwood
Derby Trolleybuses ... Colin Barker
Grimsby & Cleethorpes Trolleybuses ... Colin Barker
Huddersfield Trolleybuses ... Stephen Lockwood
Hull Trolleybuses ... Paul Morfitt and Malcolm Wells
Ipswich Trolleybuses ... Colin Barker
Mexborough & Swinton Trolleybuses ... Colin Barker
Newcastle Trolleybuses ... Stephen Lockwood
Nottinghamshire & Derbyshire Trolleybuses ... Barry M Marsden
Reading Trolleybuses ... David Hall
South Shields Trolleybuses ... Stephen Lockwood
Tees-side Trolleybuses ... Stephen Lockwood
Wolverhampton Trolleybuses 1961-67 ... Graham Sidwell
Woolwich and Dartford Trolleybuses ... Robert J Harley

Trolleybuses included in the Tramways series -
Keighley Tramways & Trolleybuses, York Tramways & Trolleybuses,
Fulwell - Home for Trams, Trolleys & Buses

TRIUMPHANT TRAMWAYS FULL COLOUR

Triumphant Tramways of England Stephen Lockwood
Blackpool * Croydon * Manchester * Midland Metro * Nottingham * Sheffield